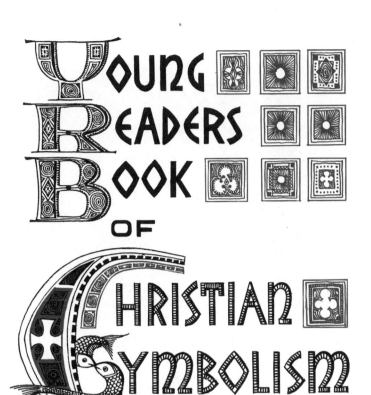

Young Readers Book of Christian Symbolism

Young Readers Book of

Christian Symbolism

Michael Daves

ILLUSTRATED BY GORDON LAITE

ABINGDON PRESS

NASHVILLE   NEW YORK

This is for Donna Michelle

CONTENTS

What Is a Symbol?

A SYMBOL IS AN OBJECT OR SIGN which stands for something else. A symbol is a visible representation of something invisible, like an idea or quality. It is often said that symbols "point beyond themselves." This means that symbols are not important in and of themselves, but they receive life from what they stand for. We need symbols. They feed our minds and spirits. They help remind us of things unseen.

Let us look at several symbols we know well.

Flying on a mast outside every school in the United States is a flag. The flag is made of pieces of material colored red, white, and blue. On the flag are fifty stars which stand for each state in the Union. But the flag is more than a piece of material. The flag represents our country, "the land of the free and the home of the brave." It reminds us of our history, our laws and freedoms. The flag "points beyond itself" to America. Congress has passed rules about the flag. The flag is to be treated with care. It should never be allowed to touch the ground. When it passes in a parade, men are supposed to take off their hats. If someone were to take an American flag, throw it on the ground and stomp it, we would be angry. He would be insulting our country if he treated the flag with such disrespect.

A handshake and kiss are symbols also. A handshake is a common way of greeting someone. It says, "I want to know you better. I want to be your friend." A kiss is a symbol of affection or love.

Another symbol is the wedding ring. It is an outward and visible sign which stands for the marriage vows a couple take to live together "for better, for worse, for richer, for poorer, in sickness and in health, 'til death us do part." The ring is not the marriage itself, but it symbolizes the marriage. The ring helps man and wife to remember the promises they have made before God.

The words printed on the pages of this book are symbols. So are the words we use in daily conversation. Words stand for what we are talking about. For example, the word "dog" is not the dog, but only stands for an animal called dog in the English language.

This book tells the story of the Christian church's symbols. It shows pictures of each symbol, and explains why the symbol is important. Symbols of the church should be treated reverently because of what they stand for.

Symbols were an important part of Christian life from the very beginning. The Old Testament prophets who told about Jesus' coming used word symbols to tell of his importance. They called him "Lamb of God," and "shepherd." Jesus himself said, "I am the Light of the World," and "I am the Bread of Life."

After Jesus' death and resurrection, Christians remembered these teachings. Artists would depict the word symbols in visual symbols—pictures. The Bible is the great source book for the visual symbols of the church. Without the word symbols of the Bible, we would not have visual symbols.

Old Testament Symbols

THE OLD TESTAMENT IS RICH WITH symbols. These symbols are not as widely used in Christian sanctuaries as New Testament symbols, but they form an important part of our history. The Old and New Testaments belong together. It is impossible to understand the New Testament without reference to the Old Testament.

The first group of symbols comes from stories in the first eleven chapters of Genesis.

A snake stands for the sinfulness of man. The ancient writer who told of man's temptation (Genesis 3) used a serpent as a symbol for evil. The serpent tempted Eve to eat the forbidden fruit. Although no one knows what fruit the writer had in mind, tradition says it was the apple. So, a snake coiled around an apple tree or around the world is a way

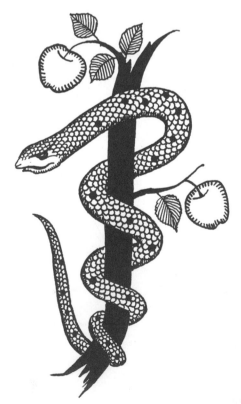

of saying "all have sinned and fallen short of the glory of God."

Another symbol is the flaming sword. When Adam and Eve ate the forbidden fruit, their relationship with God was broken. They were forced to leave the garden of Eden. "He [God] drove out the man; and at the east of the garden of Eden he placed the cherubim, and a flaming sword which turned every way, to guard the way to the tree of life." (Genesis 3:24.)

The story of the Flood and Noah's Ark is found in Genesis 6–9. Noah's Ark represents salvation. Noah and his family found safety from the flood inside the Ark. A dove with an olive branch is the symbol of peace. Noah sent out a dove to see whether the flood waters were going down (Genesis 8:8). When the dove returned with an olive leaf, Noah knew that it was safe to leave the Ark. A final symbol which comes from this story is the rainbow. The rainbow assures us of God's love and protection. The writer of this story believed that the rainbow was the sign of God's covenant with Noah and the Israelite nation (Genesis 9:13).

A tower also symbolizes man's sinfulness. In the eleventh chapter of Genesis, the writer tells that men wanted to build a tower to the heavens. He meant that people want to put their will ahead of God's will. We are self-centered and disobedient.

The second group of symbols originates from the worship of the Jewish people.

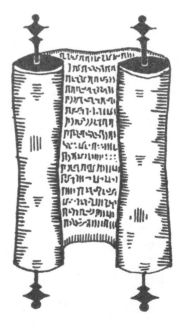

The law formed an important part of Jewish life and worship. The Jews believed that God called them to keep his law. The scroll stands for the first five books of the Old Testament. These are called the Torah, and contain the most sacred Jewish laws.

For Christians, the Ten Commandments represent the best insights of the Jewish law. We do not follow the dietary and worship rules of the Jews, but we believe the Ten Commandments help us to know God's will for our lives. The Ten Commandments are symbolized by two tablets of stone with Roman numerals numbering to ten. The Ten Commandments are found in Exodus 20:2-17.

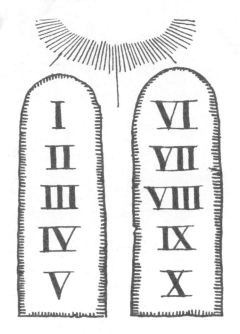

The altar of sacrifice is the main symbol of Old Testament worship. The Jews believed that God wanted them to give their lives to him. They symbolized this by sacrificing an animal, usually an ox or sheep, and by bringing the first fruits of the harvest.

The Psalmist said,
Praise the Lord with the lyre,
    make melody to him with the harp
      of ten strings!
Sing to him a new song,
    play skilfully on the strings, with
      loud shouts. (Psalms 33:2-3.)

A picture of the harp or lyre stands for praise and worship. This symbol is sometimes seen on choir benches.

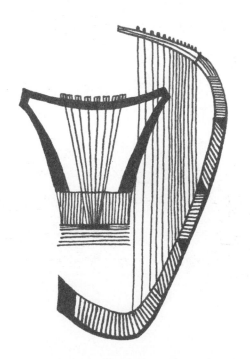

A censer contains sweet-smelling incense which was burned in the worship service. The sweet smell helped the people worship God by employing their sense of smell in the service. The burning censer stands for worship and adoration.

The last symbol for Jewish worship is the Menorah, or seven-branched candlestick. The light of the Menorah symbolized the presence of God in the temple. So long as the temple was used as a place of worship, the Menorah was kept burning. Today, in every synagogue, one or two Menorahs are always placed on the altar. The flaming Menorah is a frequent symbol of the Jewish faith itself.

The third group of symbols refers to characters of the Old Testament.

Adam's sign is the shovel because he was told by God that he must earn his food by the sweat of his brow (Genesis 3:19).

Eve's sign is a distaff, which is a staff used for holding flax or wool in spinning. Since spinning was a woman's job, the distaff is a good symbol for Eve.

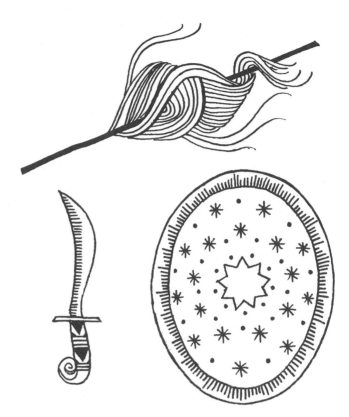

Abraham is symbolized by a sacrificial knife, which refers to his willingness to kill his son Isaac at God's command (Genesis 22:1-14). God's promise to Abraham is represented by a blue shield with many stars. The large star stands for the best promise of all, the Messiah.

Jacob's family is symbolized by a sun and full moon for Jacob and his wife. Twelve stars stand for their twelve sons.

Joseph was the most famous of the sons of Jacob. His father gave him a many colored coat (Genesis 37:3-4), which is his symbol.

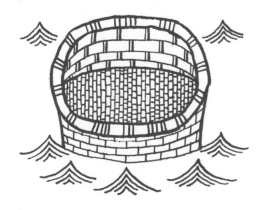

Moses is remembered by two signs. One is a basket of bulrushes. Shortly after he was born, his mother put him in a basket and floated him down the river. In this way, she saved him from Pharaoh who sought

17

to kill all the Hebrew babies. Moses was found by Pharaoh's daughter, who took pity on him and adopted him as her own (Exodus 2:1-10). The other sign associated with Moses is the burning bush out of which God called him to be a leader of his people (Exodus 3:1-12).

King David is symbolized by a harp because he was a skilled musician (I Samuel 16:16-19), and by a lion which stands for his bravery as a shepherd boy.

Joshua, the great military leader, has for his sign a sword and trumpet. The wall of Jericho fell when his army blew trumpets (Joshua 6:1-21).

Solomon, one of the wisest Jewish kings, is best known for building a magnificent temple in Jerusalem (II Chronicles 3:1-17). Solomon's sign is a model of the temple.

Ruth's sign is one wisp of wheat. She gleaned the wheat in the field of Boaz (Ruth 2:1-7).

Elijah, the prophet, is pictured riding on a flaming chariot. This refers to an account from II Kings 2. Elijah and Elisha were walking and talking together. Suddenly, a chariot of fire and horses of fire separated the two. "And Elijah went up by a whirlwind into heaven." (II Kings 2:11*b*.)

Amos, the prophet, is remembered by a single shepherd's staff because he was called to be a prophet from the sheep herds of Tekoa. (Amos 1:1.)

Finally, we want to look at what some people have called the Old Testament cross. It is interesting to know that a form of the cross was a worship symbol long before Jesus came.

Moses ordered the children of Israel to kill lambs, dip bunches of hyssop in the blood and paint a sign upon the doorposts of their huts. Moses had talked with God, and learned that this night the Lord would slay the firstborn of the Egyptians because Pharaoh had failed to let the Israelites leave Egypt. The Israelite children would be saved if they painted this sign on their huts.

According to tradition, this strange sign was a cross. It hardly looked like a cross, but more like the letter T. We call it the Tau cross, taken from the Greek name for the letter T. This cross is believed to be the cross on which Moses raised up the bronze serpent (Numbers 21:8-9).

Whenever we see a Tau cross, we should remember that God revealed his ways to men in Old Testament times. His coming to them was a preparation for his coming in Jesus Christ. The Tau, or Old Testament cross, is a strong link between the Jewish and Christian traditions.

Symbols in the Church

IN THE EARLY DAYS OF THE CHURCH, the Roman empire persecuted the Christians. During this period, symbols served as a way to protect Christians from discovery. Since only Christians knew the meaning of their symbols, they sometimes could use them as a protection from persecution. Symbols were used often as a test of identity.

Later, the church became accepted. Great cathedrals were built. Kings were baptized, and their people followed them. Almost every family could boast of a son who entered the priesthood. The church had power and riches. It was a far cry from the early days of Roman persecution. Still, symbols were vital in the life of the church.

Printing had not been invented. Books had to be copied by hand—a long, hard process. Very few copies of the Bible were available. Besides, only a small number of people were able to read. Priests were the most educated men in the community. They tried to interpret the Bible to the people. One way they helped tell about Jesus was through visible symbols. Priests led peasants who could not read to beautiful stained-glass windows. They pointed to the symbols and told stories about them. In this way, the peasants learned about the Christian faith.

As time passed, symbols began to be misused. The church became lax in teaching. Ignorant peasants believed that the symbol itself contained the power, instead of standing for the power of God. The masses believed that a cross held magic power. They thought they could ward off evil simply by carrying a cross. To raise money, the church sold pieces of paper called indulgences. It was believed that a person did not need

to repent honestly of his sins, for he could buy an indulgence. The church lost the power it once had.

Many faithful people were disturbed about the church's life. They felt that it had strayed from the plain teachings of the Bible. Two such men were Martin Luther, a German, and John Calvin, a Frenchman. These men, along with others, set about to reform the church. Luther translated the Bible into the language of the people so they could read it for themselves. He said salvation came through faith in God alone and not by performing good deeds. Calvin, even more than Luther, set about to change the church's worship. Calvin believed that the symbols had become a substitute for God and were evil. He felt the best way to save the people from worshiping symbols was to destroy the symbols.

Thanks to Martin Luther, John Calvin, and others like them, we no longer accept symbols as substitutes for God. Today the church is able to use its symbols not as things to worship but as aids to worship. Christians worship God alone, but our visual symbols help us to worship him. Today we do not believe the best way to prevent misunderstanding a symbol is to destroy it. We believe that people should be taught the meaning of symbols as outward and visible signs of the way God comes to us inwardly.

The Cross

YOU MAY FIND IT DIFFICULT TO understand why the cross is the chief symbol of the church. The cross reminds us of a very sad time, and we usually want to forget sad times. Jesus' enemies had him arrested. He was led to Caiaphas, the high priest. "Are you the Christ, the Son of God?" Caiaphas asked. When Jesus replied he was, Caiaphas became angry. He thought Jesus was blaspheming, and that he should be put to death. Since the Romans occupied Palestine, only the Roman government could sentence a man to death. So Jesus was taken to the Roman governor, Pilate. Although Pilate didn't find any fault with Jesus, he bowed to the wishes of an angry crowd and sentenced Jesus to death. Jesus was forced to carry his cross to a place outside Jerusalem known as Golgotha, which means "place of the skull." There he was nailed to the cross. After six hours of suffering, he died. Crucifixion was a painful way of executing the worst criminals.

We are sorry that Jesus died on the cross. But Christians remember the crucifixion with thanksgiving and joy, which overcomes sadness. Soon after Jesus' death, his disciples became convinced that their Master was alive again. They realized that he died because he wanted to show them how much God loved them. He died so that we might live. This, too, is hard for us to understand, but it is like a soldier in battle being shot dead as he shields the body of a wounded friend. The cross helps us remember God's love for us as shown in Jesus Christ.

There are more than fifty forms of the cross used in Christian art. Let's look at five of the most popular.

The Latin cross is best known because it was the kind of cross on which Christ was crucified. Protestants have an empty cross which symbolizes that although Christ died, he is alive forevermore. Some Christians display a cross on which there is a figure representing Christ. They believe this helps recall his suffering. Such a cross is called a crucifix.

In the early days of the church, people made the sign of the Latin cross when they worshiped. They traced a small cross on the forehead with the thumb of their right hands. About seven hundred years ago, worshipers began making a much larger sign of the cross. They traced the cross from forehead to breast, then from left to right. Some Christians

still make the sign of the cross after they pray. It is a physical way of remembering that Christians are under the sign of the cross and should follow Christ's command to "take up your cross and follow me."

For hundreds of years, church buildings were patterned after the Latin cross. The world's most beautiful churches are built on what is called a cruciform plan, meaning they are shaped like the Latin cross. If you lay this book down on a table and look at the Latin cross, you are able to get an idea of what the building looks like. Pretend you are high in the air, flying over a cruciform church. The nave is the area which extends from the cross arms to the bottom. The people worship here. The arms are suggested in the cruciform plan by side extensions called transepts. Usually, people are seated in the transepts and face the front of the church—the top of the cross, as you look at it. The area above the

26

cross arms is the space reserved for the minister and choir. The pulpit (the stand from which the minister preaches) and the lectern (the stand from which the Bible is read) are immediately above the arms on either side. The altar (where the bread and wine for Communion are placed) is at the very top of the cross in the center.

A variation of the Latin cross is known as the Celtic cross. The Celts were an ancient people, tall and blond. The best examples of the Celtic cross have been found in Ireland where a part of this ancient race lived. People who have studied the history of crosses say that the Celtic cross commonly marked graves in Irish and British cemeteries. The custom spread to America in the early days. Why is the Celtic cross in cemeteries? It is because the circle

27

stands for eternal life. The circle helps us remember that the dead are still God's children and, although they are not with us any longer, they are with God.

In the eleventh century, Christians went in groups to visit the Holy Sepulcher—the place where it is believed Christ was buried. They were called pilgrims. On the way, the pilgrims were often attacked by robber bands. Imagine their joy when concerned laymen organized the Knights of St. John to protect them. Enemies of the Christians, the Turks, banished the knights from the island of Rhodes, but Charles V let them live on the island of Malta. From there, they carried on their work of protecting pilgrims on their way to Jerusalem. Emblazoned on their bright shields was a cross known today as the Maltese cross. The name came from the island where the knights settled. The Maltese cross differs from both the Latin and Celtic

crosses, appearing to be four spearheads meeting in the center. Eight outer points stand for the Beatitudes, which you may find in Matthew 5:3-11.

Other than the Latin cross, the Anchor cross is the oldest design. First-century Christians carved it on the walls of the catacombs. Like the fish symbol, the Anchor cross was meant to hide its true identity to all but Christian eyes. The pagan who saw an Anchor cross would see only an anchor; the Christian would see a cross. The Anchor cross also reminded Christians that Jesus' death gave them life. It probably refers directly to Hebrews 6:19. In this Scripture, hope is described as "a sure and steadfast anchor of the soul." The Christian can hope because Jesus Christ came.

Sometimes you will see in stained-glass windows a Latin cross planted on top of a globe. This is called the

Cross of Triumph, and it means that the Gospel has been preached all over the world. Brave missionaries, following Jesus' command "to go into all the world," have endured terrible dangers to help people in the name of Jesus. The Cross of Triumph makes us think of boys and girls going to a mission school in India, a woman receiving surgery in a new hospital in the Congo, and Christians building a church in Sumatra. Isn't it amazing to think that Christianity has grown from tiny Palestine to include every country in the world?

The cross has inspired Christians in every age to speak and write beautiful words of devotion. One was John Bowring. Active in British politics, he was the consul general of Hong Kong over a hundred years ago. The words he wrote were set to music, and we sing them today. The first verse goes like this:

> In the cross of Christ I glory,
>   Towering o'er the wrecks of time;
> All the light of sacred story
>   Gathers round its head sublime.

Symbols of Holy Week

THE WEEK BEFORE EASTER DAY IS A very special time of year when we think about Jesus' suffering and death. It is known as Holy Week. The Gospel writers felt the week was so important that they carefully described the details of what happened to Jesus and his disciples. It is exciting to read the stories directly from the Gospels of Matthew, Mark, Luke, and John. The symbols of Jesus' last week on earth came from these stories.

The church observes Jesus' entry into Jerusalem on the Sunday before Easter, which is called Palm Sunday. Jesus rode into the city on an ass. Some say that he did this to show that he was humble, since the ass is a beast of burden. However, the main reason was to tell everyone that he was God's Chosen One. The prophet Zechariah had written centuries before, "Lo, your king comes to you; triumphant and victorious is he, humble and riding on an ass" (Zechariah 9:9). His followers welcomed him by spreading some of their clothing and palm branches on the road. Children and adults walked close to Jesus, shouting. Palm branches waved in the air. It was a happy time. Because of Zechariah's words, Jesus' coming into Jerusalem is called the "Triumphal Entry."

Some churches pin small palm leaves to the clothing of the worshipers on Palm Sunday to help them remember this moment. Palm leaves are the symbol for the Triumphal Entry. Hymn writers, too, help us remember. A Christian leader who lived long ago in France, Theodolph of Orleans, sang,

> All glory, laud and honor,
>   To Thee, Redeemer, King,
> To whom the lips of children
>   Made sweet hosannas ring.
> Thou art the King of Israel,
>   Thou David's royal Son,
> Who in the Lord's Name comest,
>   The King and Blessed One.

Later in the week—on Thursday evening—Jesus took his disciples to an upper room for a meal. The Gospel writer, John, tells a lovely story about this night. After eating, Jesus tied a towel around his waist. He poured water from a pitcher into a basin. Then, he began washing the disciples' feet. Jesus was their master, but he was performing the task of a slave!

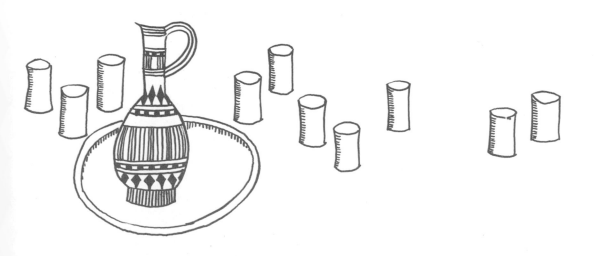

It didn't seem right for him to do this. So Peter said, "You'll never wash my feet!" But Jesus insisted, and Peter let him. Afterward, Jesus told them he washed their feet to teach them a lesson. No one should fail to do the lowliest tasks for people in need. The basin and pitcher as symbols of humility come from this story.

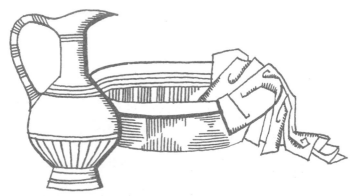

The first three Gospels—Matthew, Mark, and Luke—record another event that happened during the meal on Thursday evening. As Jesus and the disciples were eating, Jesus took bread, gave thanks, broke it, and gave the pieces to others. "This is my body," he said. Then, he took a cup of wine and said, "This is my blood." He commanded them to eat and drink. Since that night, Christians have shared together in remembrance of Christ a meal known as the Lord's Supper. A cup stands for the Lord's Supper, which every church observes today, and for the last supper Jesus had with his disciples long ago.

Sometimes you will see a cup pictured with a cross. After that last supper, Jesus and his disciples went to a nearby garden where grapes were grown—the Garden of Gethsemane. Jesus went there to pray. He knew that his enemies were powerful, and they would soon capture him. He needed courage to face the dark days ahead. He prayed, "My Father, if it be possible, let this cup pass from me; nevertheless not what I will, but as thou wilt." (Matthew 26:39) Jesus did not want to die, but he was willing to die if God's purpose of love could be served by his death. Jesus' cup, or task, was his cross. So, cup and cross stand for Jesus' obeying God's will for his life.

Jesus barely finished his prayer and returned to his disciples when the Garden of Gethsemane rustled with the sound of feet. Soldiers had come to arrest Jesus. One of Jesus' own followers, Judas, had told Jesus' enemies where Jesus might be found. For this information, they paid him thirty pieces of silver. A purse with thirty coins is the symbol for Judas' evil deed.

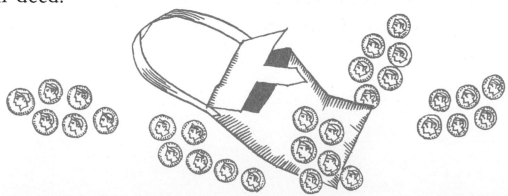

When Judas saw Jesus with the rest of the disciples, he told the soldiers that he would let them know which one was Jesus by kissing him. Kissing was a common form of greeting in those days—as handshaking is today. Judas stepped out of the shadows and kissed Jesus on the cheek.

Four symbols represent the arrest of Jesus: lantern, torch, sword and staff, sword and ear. Each comes from John's story of the arrest. In the eighteenth chapter of the Gospel of John, the Evangelist wrote, "So Judas, procuring a band of soldiers and some officers from the chief priests and the Pharisees, went there with lanterns and torches and weapons." The sword and staff represent the weapons mentioned by John. A few verses later, John gives the incident on which the sword and ear symbol is based: "Then Simon Peter, having a sword, drew it and struck the high priest's slave and cut off his right ear. The slave's name was Malchus. Jesus said to Peter, 'Put your sword into its sheath; shall I not drink the cup which the Father has given me?'"

After Jesus was arrested, the disciples ran away. They were afraid. Peter slipped inside the court of the high priest's house where Jesus had been taken. He wanted to hear some news from the palace guards who were warming themselves beside a small fire.

Peter sat close to the fire. His thoughts were far away. One woman looked closely at Peter in the firelight. "Aren't you one of Jesus' disciples?" Her question cut through him like a steel knife.

"No, no, I'm not," Peter said. "You must have me mixed up with someone else." He left the fireside, starting toward the gate. The woman followed him. She said to the others standing around, "This man is one of them." Again, Peter denied it.

One of the crowd came up to him. "You are one of his men. You come from Galilee."

Peter shot back with hot words. He was afraid for his very life. "I do not know the man, I tell you!" he said angrily, trying hard to hide his fear.

In that moment the crowing of a rooster cut the night air. No one seemed to hear it but Peter. Then, the rooster crowed a second time. The words of Jesus came rushing back to Peter's mind, "Before the cock crows twice, you will deny me three times." And he had! Overcome by remorse, Peter's eyes filled with tears. His knees became so weak that he could hardly leave the courtyard. All he could think of was the rooster's crowing and his denial.

This sad story of Peter's denial of Christ is preserved in Christian art by the symbol of a rooster crowing.

Jesus was tried, found guilty, and sentenced to death. On Friday, Jesus was crucified. He suffered on the cross for hours while his enemies taunted him. The best-known symbol of the crucifixion is the Latin cross. However, three other symbols stand for the crucifixion and refer to events which took place that day.

There is the crown of thorns and the three nails. The soldiers, making fun of Jesus, placed a crown of thorns on his head. "He is King of the Jews!" they laughed. The nails were driven into Jesus' hands and feet.

> See, from His head, His hands, His feet,
> Sorrow and love flow mingled down:
> Did e'er such love and sorrow meet,
> Or thorns compose so rich a crown?

As Jesus was dying on the cross, the four soldiers who were in charge of his crucifixion began dividing up his clothing. They came to his robe and found that it had no seam. Not wanting to tear it, they decided to throw dice, the winner to get Jesus' robe. So another crucifixion symbol is the seamless robe and three dice.

Symbols of Resurrection

THE DISCIPLES SAW THEIR LORD crucified. They took his body down from the cross and laid it reverently in a tomb. He was dead. Their hearts ached. They cried lonely tears. They felt empty inside. Then, the third day after his death, Jesus appeared to those who loved him. Excitement spread through their ranks. Their sorrow turned to shouting. "The Lord is risen!" one disciple said when he met another one. The reply came back, "He is risen indeed!" Jesus' victory over death and his renewed fellowship with the disciples is called the resurrection. Christians rejoice at all times over Christ's resurrection, but it is particularly remembered Easter Day.

Symbols of resurrection are glad announcements of the news that Christ is risen. All of them are taken from nature. Bright-colored and beautiful, these symbols fill us with joy when we look at them.

The most familiar resurrection symbol is the lily. Children's choirs carry lilies on Easter Day and place them at the front of the church so the congregation can see their

beauty. Pictures of lilies are seen in stained-glass windows. Not all lilies are white, but they are always pictured white in Christian art because the color white stands for purity, joy, light.

Why is the lily an Easter symbol? Because of the way it grows. You put an ugly brown bulb, seemingly without life, in the soil. From this bulb comes a new bulb. Then, stem, leaves and flowers, all rise above the soil. Even though the bulb decays— the bulb standing for the earthly body—new life springs from it. Lilies bloom in the spring, close to Easter.

A little known resurrection symbol is the pomegranate. It is a small shrub which produces round juicy fruit about the size of an orange. A valuable food for ages, pomegranates are mentioned often in the Old Testament. The pomegranate is a resurrection symbol because its fruit bursts open from the pressure of seeds. It stands for the power of new life.

Everyone loves to watch butterflies gracefully flying in the breeze. But not everyone knows that the butterfly is also a resurrection symbol. This is because in an early stage of growth, the butterfly grows in a smooth, hard shell which often rests on a leaf or branch. The shell appears dead. But inside the hard shell (which is called the chrysalis) a butterfly is growing. In about two weeks, the butterfly breaks out of the chrysalis. When its wings dry, it flies away—free from its prison.

A bird known as the peacock is a symbol of the resurrection. The peacock is one of the most famous birds in the world. King Solomon brought peacocks to Palestine. Long ago, they were taken to China, where they became a symbol of fire and fortune. Alexander the Great brought peacocks to Europe. People kept the peacock as a pet to decorate their houses. The most gorgeous part of the peacock is the tail feathers. These tail feathers will drop off (called molting), but new feathers—more attractive than before—will grow to take their place. In this, we see new life coming from death.

Another bird, the phoenix, is also a symbol of the resurrection. In Arabia, stories were told about this bird —stories that are like fairy tales. The word phoenix may have come from a Greek word which means date-palm tree. The Arabians used the ashes of burned date-palm trees as fertilizer for seeds. This may be the reason the story was told about a bird that flew from the ashes of the fire in which it had been burned. The phoenix is shown with its wings raised in flight, coming out of flames. Once dead, the bird lives again.

43

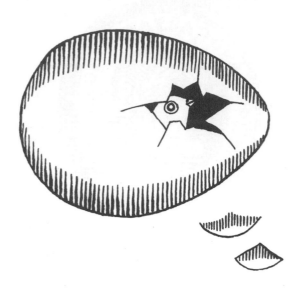

The egg is a resurrection symbol because it contains new life. When a hen lays an egg, inside is a material which will make a tiny baby chick if it is ever hatched. The new life comes into the world when the chick breaks out of the egg and breathes the air of the world around him. The chick pecks on the shell until he finds release. This symbol is related to Christ's resurrection in much the same way as the butterfly.

Fish

WHEN THE CHURCH WAS YOUNG, the Roman empire ruled a large part of the world. The empire was governed by an emperor, whom the Romans worshiped as a god. They bowed down to him, and burned incense in his honor. Christians refused to do this. For them, there was only one God—the God who was revealed in Jesus Christ. Since they believed in following Christ's way of peace, they also refused service in the Roman army. The pagan Romans regarded them as dangerous.

Rome persecuted the Christians. Many were thrown to the lions and made to fight animals in front of large crowds. It is said that the emperor Nero set fire to Rome, and blamed it on the Christians. A new wave of persecution swept Rome under his reign. It was a dangerous time to be a follower of Jesus. Many Christian families were separated from one another, with children watching sadly as their fathers were taken to prison.

Naturally, Christians tried to protect themselves from the Romans. They met in secret, often in underground burial vaults known as the catacombs. Sometimes, they would meet in a fellow Christian's house. There were no church buildings then, as there are today.

One way the Christians avoided arrest was by using the fish symbol. The fish was a secret code. When the pagans painted a fish on their houses, it meant that there was a funeral banquet inside. However, when a Christian displayed the symbol, it meant that a worship service would be held that night in secret. What a clever trick! The pagan passing by a Christian house thought that a funeral banquet was being held, while the Christian knew it was a church meeting.

Here is a story that illustrates another way the fish symbol

was used. Two strangers, both slaves, met on a street. They began talking about the day's work. As they spoke, one began moving his right foot slowly in a circle, drawing a fish in the sand. The other glanced down. A flash of recognition crossed his face. Smiling, he drew a fish. Then, the two clasped hands. No longer strangers, they were friends in Christ. If the other slave had been a pagan, the Christian would have been protected from discovery and perhaps from arrest for his tracing of the fish would have held no meaning for the non-Christian.

Why did the Christians use a fish as the sign of their faith? Because the Greek letters ΙΧΘΥΕ which happen to spell fish are the first letters of the five Greek words meaning "Jesus Christ, Son of God, Savior." In English those five first letters look something like this:

I stands for the Greek word for Jesus.

CH stands for the Greek word for Christ.

TH stands for the Greek word for God.

U stands for the Greek word for Son.

S stands for the Greek word for Savior.

The fish was also carved on the burial vaults of Christians. In the catacombs, the fish was often shown with a basket on its back, the basket containing wine and bread; or the fish was shown on a three-legged table. When pictured this way, the fish tells us that Christ comes to us in the Lord's Supper. Some Christians even carried small stone images of the fish to identify themselves!

During the Roman persecution, Polycarp, the Bishop of Smyrna, was hauled before a state official. The official said, "Swear, and I will release you. Curse the Christ!" The old man stood straight and said, "I have served him for eighty-six years, and he has done me no wrong. How can I curse my king who saved me?" Refusing to deny Christ, Polycarp was killed.

Whenever we see the fish, we think of Jesus Christ. We also remember thousands of his brave followers like Polycarp, who suffered pain and death because they dared to believe in Jesus Christ, Son of God, Savior.

ΙΧΘΥΣ

Lamb of God

LONG BEFORE JESUS WAS BORN, THE prophet Isaiah wrote about the sufferings of a man who would come to save Israel. In beautiful poetry, he said that this man would take the sins of the people on himself. The one of whom Isaiah wrote came to be known as the Suffering Servant. Isaiah likens his obedience to a lamb which goes quietly to be slaughtered.

John the Baptist, a prophet in the time of Jesus, told people that the man Isaiah spoke about was soon to come. One day John was preaching by the Jordan River. Jesus walked from the crowd. John saw him and cried to the people, "Behold, the Lamb of God, who takes away the sins of the world!" He believed Jesus was the fulfillment of Isaiah's hopes.

Lambs were favorite pets of children in Jewish homes. Every Jewish family bought two lambs at Passover time. They would kill one and eat it at the meal which celebrated the freeing of their forefathers from the Egyptians. The other lamb became a household pet. The sheep would sleep with the children, eat green grass from their hands, and drink cool water from their cups. Lambs were gentle and harmless.

A lamb is a good symbol for Jesus Christ. A lamb was always

obedient to the shepherd. The shepherd would not need to shout at the lamb. He would quietly tell the lamb where to go, guiding him gently with his staff. Jesus was obedient to God's will for his life, praying to his Father, "Not my will, but thine be done." A lamb was killed on the altar of the temple as an offering to God. It may be hard to understand why in ancient times the Jews would kill an animal in their worship, but they

thought that offering a lamb was one way to please God. Jesus, as the Lamb of God, is an offering God makes to man. We believe that Jesus in his life, death, and resurrection takes our sin on himself. We believe that God shows his love for us in Jesus Christ.

Christian art shows the Lamb in two positions.

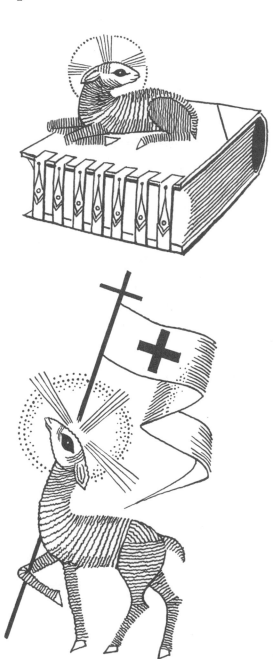

In one, the Lamb is lying on the Book of Seven Seals. The writer of Revelation believed this book contained the destiny of man, and only the Lamb could break its seals. When the Lamb of God is seen lying down, we ought to think of the death of Jesus.

The Lamb of God is also shown standing, carrying the resurrection banner. The Lamb standing signifies Jesus' victory over death. The banner, standing for Christ's body, is white. The staff is shaped like a cross, reminding us of his death on the cross. The banner also bears a cross, always colored red. A three-rayed nimbus (cloud) around the Lamb's head stands for divinity.

There are many carvings of the Lamb of God in the Roman catacombs, the dark underground burial vaults where the first-century Christians worshiped. Along with two other early symbols, the Anchor cross and the fish, the Lamb of God helped the Christians to be aware of the Risen Lord's Presence.

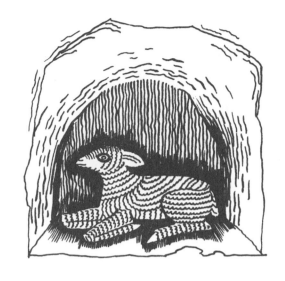

When Jesus told people he was like a good shepherd, they knew what he meant. Throughout Israel's long history, the shepherd occupied a very important place. He was respected by all the community, as doctors, lawyers, businessmen, and ministers are today. Because he spent so much time alone with his herd in nature, people thought of the shepherd as a man close to God. Some of Israel's heroes—Moses, David, and Amos—were shepherds. The Old Testament writers speak of God as a good shepherd. The writer of the twenty-third psalm began by saying,

> The Lord is my shepherd, I shall not want;
>   he makes me lie down in green pastures.
> He leads me beside still waters;
>   he restores my soul.
> He leads me in paths of righteousness
>   for his name's sake.

Early artists had the Scriptures before them when they painted Jesus as the good shepherd. The symbol was usually of a young man carrying a sheep on his shoulder. The young man was strong and muscular, symbolizing ability to defend the sheep from harm. Isn't this a good way to think of Jesus?

Once a class of children went on a tour of several churches. In one was a stained-glass window over twelve feet tall. Jesus was shown with a lamb in his arms, followed by sheep. "What do you think that means?" the children were asked. The class thought a moment, then Patti answered, "It means that Jesus cares for his children like a shepherd cares for his sheep." She was right. Jesus loves us more than we can possibly imagine. Long ago, Augustine said, "He loves us as if there were but one of us to love."

Good Shepherd

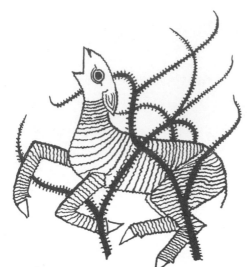

STEPHEN WAS A YOUNG SHEPHERD who tended sheep outside Bethlehem many years ago. Once he discovered one of his sheep missing. Stephen could hardly believe it, for he had kept careful watch all night. Counting again, he came up with the same number: ninety-nine, one short. "I must find the lost sheep," said Stephen, "or he will be killed by a wolf."

So Stephen set out to find the lost sheep. He searched for hours, retracing the land where the herd had grazed. Holding his hand over his eyes to ward off the rays of the sun, he looked in every direction: north, south, east, west, then south again. A quarter-mile away, he saw a bit of white against the brown earth. He started to run south. About halfway, Stephen could see the sheep, caught in the briars. Releasing it, he carried the animal home on his back.

When Stephen came home, he called his friends and neighbors together for a celebration. The young shepherd was so happy because he had found his lost sheep.

You remember Jesus told a story like this. You can find it in the fifteenth chapter of Luke. Like the shepherd searching

for even one stray sheep, Jesus would not be happy until every person knew and loved God.

Another time, Jesus told his friends, "I am the good shepherd. The good shepherd lays down his life for the sheep." (John 10:11) In Jesus' day, shepherds often gave their lives to protect the sheep from angry wolf packs. Jesus, the Good Shepherd, died because he wanted to help us lead better lives.

Crown

THE YEAR WAS 1716. THE PASTOR of the church in the village of Ystad, Sweden, was singing the first hymn along with his congregation. Glancing up from the hymnal, he saw some people entering late. He looked a second time at the latecomers. It could not be! But it was! King Charles XII of Sweden, the great warrior king, was taking his place among the worshipers.

The presence of such royalty was a complete surprise to everyone. When the time came for the sermon, the pastor felt that he should not preach the sermon he had planned for that Sunday. Instead, he spent the time telling about the greatness of King Charles.

Some months later, King Charles sent the church a gift. It was a crucifix. Enclosed was a note which read: "This is to hang on the pillar opposite the pulpit, so that all who stand there will be reminded of their proper subject." The crucifix hangs there to this very day.

King Charles attended church that Sunday to hear about the King Jesus Christ, not about himself. His gift, the cross, was a way of telling the pastor and congregation of the Ystad church that Jesus Christ is King of kings; that Jesus Christ

should be honored above the kings and great men of the world.

Christian art has a symbol which reminds Christians of the great truth that Christ is king. It is the crown. Placed on the head of a person, the crown stands for authority, royalty, power, dominion. When we see a crown pictured on a stained-glass window, in a book, or on a wall, it says to us, "Your final loyalty is to Jesus Christ. Jesus Christ is your king. You are his subject. You must be obedient to him."

Putting Jesus Christ above all kings and authorities can be dangerous. It may lead to imprisonment and death. In 1933, Hitler came to power in Germany. He believed that the state should tell the church what to do. Hitler felt every pastor should speak in favor of the Nazi government and its warlike policies.

Many German pastors did not agree with Hitler and refused to cooperate. One such pastor was named Dietrich Bonhoeffer. He believed he must serve God first. He spoke out against Hitler. Defying the government, he became head of a theological seminary, where men were prepared for the ministry.

War came in 1939. Bonhoeffer was opposed to the war. Hitler would not let him teach, nor have any of his writings published. Finally, Bonhoeffer joined in a plot to overthrow Hitler. He believed the dictator was wrecking the country and was against God. Sadly, the plot failed.

Dietrich Bonhoeffer was arrested and imprisoned in 1943. In prison, he wrote about what it meant to follow Christ as King. He helped his fellow prisoners. He prayed with them. He preached to them. He taught them from the Bible. Finally, he was sentenced to death. As he walked down the hall to be hanged, he said, "This is the end, but for me the beginning of life."

On April 9, 1945, this brave follower of Christ was put to death.

Dietrich Bonhoeffer's example helps us to be better followers of Christ, placing him first in our lives as our King.

Monograms of Jesus Christ

A MONOGRAM IS A COMBINATION OF letters representing a person's name. You have seen monogrammed handkerchiefs and stationery. From earliest times, the church has employed monograms to stand for the name of Jesus Christ. Some of these monograms are very familiar and are used perhaps more than any symbol other than the cross.

The oldest monogram for Jesus Christ is the Chi-Rho. This monogram is formed by placing the Greek letters X (chi) and P (rho) together. X and P are the first two letters of the Greek word for Christ. When spelled in Greek capital letters the word for Christ looked like this:

ΧΡΙΣΤΟΣ

Constantine the Great put the Chi-Rho on the banners of his army as he marched against the Roman Emperor Maxentius. Constantine was the first royal convert to Christianity. There is a legend about his use of the Chi-Rho. As his army was settled down by the Tiber, Constantine saw a shining Chi-Rho symbol in the sky. He also saw the words: *In hoc signo vinces,* Latin for "in this sign thou shalt conquer." Constantine was disturbed for he did not know what the sign meant. He fell into a troubled sleep. Upon awaking, he knew that the sign in the sky stood for Christ. Constantine ordered his men to paint the symbol on their standards and shields before going into battle. The battle was won. Constantine was the sole ruler of the Western Empire. Under this good, wise emperor, the persecution of the Christians was ended.

Letters which look like an A and an upside down U are the first and last letters in the Greek alphabet—the alpha and omega (A and Ω). Always the alpha and omega should be shown with one of the symbols representing Jesus Christ. When used alone, they are merely the first and last letters of the Greek alphabet. When seen with a symbol for Jesus Christ, they stand for Christ, "the first and the last, the beginning and the end" (Revelation 22:13).

IHS is another monogram for Jesus Christ. There are several interpretations of what this monogram means. Some say that the symbol is an abbreviation for Latin words which mean "Jesus, Savior of Men." Others believe that the IHS means "I [Christ] have suffered." The real explanation is that the letters IHΣ are the first three letters of the Greek word for Jesus (IHΣOYΣ). When knowledge of the Greek language declined, the church substituted the Latin letter S for the Greek letter sigma. Sometimes, we see the symbol in the original Greek spelling, IHΣ.

The next monogram—INRI—dates back to the crucifixion of Jesus. Pilate ordered an inscription to be placed above Jesus' head in three languages—Greek, Latin, and Hebrew. This monogram, INRI, stands for the inscription in Latin, *Iesus Nazarenus Rex Iudaeorum*. This Latin phrase translates: Jesus of Nazareth, King of the Jews.

Candle and Torch

THE CANDLELIGHTING SERVICE AT Christmas is perhaps the most beautiful of the whole year. Favorite Christmas carols are sung; the children's choir sings; scriptures telling about Jesus' birth are read. At the climax of the service, the minister lights the candles of the ushers. In turn, the ushers light the candles of the persons sitting on the end of the pews. This light is passed from person to person until every candle in the sanctuary is lit. The candles are raised, and the congregation sings a carol.

Why are candles good symbols for worship? Is it only because they make a pretty light? No. We use candles in our worship because the candle is a symbol for Jesus Christ.

When the church was persecuted by the Romans, they held services in the dark, damp catacombs below the city. People were buried in the catacombs. Often, the bread and wine for Holy Communion would be placed on top of a tomb. Since it was dark, candles would be lighted so the congregation could see. At first, candles simply served the same purpose as electric-light bulbs—to give light for people to see.

However, a significance was soon attached to the candles. The early Christians remembered the words of Jesus, "I am the

light of the world." They knew that he had caused light to shine in the darkness of their lives, giving them hope and courage. When candles were lit, Christians thought of Jesus as the "Light of the World." The custom continues today.

Two candles are placed on the altar or communion table to remind Christians that Jesus was a man, but at the same time God was with him in a special way.

The torch is a closely related symbol. Every person who believes that Jesus Christ is the Light of the World is symbolized by a torch. The torch recalls this saying of Jesus: "Let your light so shine before men, that they may see your good works and give glory to your Father who is in heaven." (Matthew 5:16.) Christ has given the Christian light. Our calling is to share this light with other people through deeds of thoughtfulness, love, and consideration. In ancient Greece, the torch was carried in long relay races. One runner handed it to another runner. As the Greek runner gave the torch to his teammate, one generation of Christians passes on the Christian faith to another.

Dove

"WHAT SYMBOL DID YOU LIKE best?" Mr. Jackson asked his class after they had toured the sanctuary.

"I liked the dove," said Tommy.

Everyone knew why. Tommy lived near the edge of town. In his back yard, a large shed was enclosed by chicken wire. Inside were pigeons. Tommy raised pigeons for pets. A dove is an untamed pigeon.

"Does anyone know what the dove stands for?" asked Mr. Jackson.

No one answered. There was a long silence until Mr. Jackson said: "If you turn to the stories of Jesus' baptism in the Gospel, you will find that the writers said the 'Holy Spirit descended like a dove from heaven.' From your study in church school, you remember that the Holy Spirit is the active presence of God. So, when Jesus was baptized, God anointed him for his work. He came to be with Jesus in a special way.

"Christians believe that God is active today through the Holy Spirit. The Bible teaches us that the Holy Spirit guides us in truth, comforts us when we are sad, strengthens us to lead the good life, and helps the church tell the good news about Jesus. The Holy Spirit is God with us now.

"The dove is one of the best-known symbols for the Holy Spirit because of the Gospel stories of Jesus' baptism. When we see the dove, we are reminded of Jesus' baptism. When we are baptized with water, we follow Jesus in baptism. We are brought into the fellowship of the church. We ask that the Holy Spirit might be active in our lives.

"You also ought to notice that the dove is always pointing downward, which symbolizes that God comes to us. The circle around the dove's head stands for divinity."

Seven-Tongued Flame

THE CAMPERS SAT AROUND A LARGE fire, singing one of the favorite songs learned during their week at church camp, "Spirit of the living God." Every eye was trained on the fire, which made a loud crackling sound as it burned the wood and brush. The fire was fascinating. It leaped into the dark night, driving back the darkness. It caused strange, dancing patches of light to appear on the faces of those who sat around it. The fire felt warm against the cold night air. The campers felt God very close, and they were thankful for this experience around the fire.

A seven-tongued flame is a very old symbol of the Holy Spirit. It is based on a story from the second chapter of Acts. The disciples had gathered after Jesus' death and resurrection. It was the day of Pentecost, a Jewish festival which celebrated God's giving the law to Moses. Suddenly, they felt they were not alone. God in Jesus Christ was with them again. In writing about the experience, Luke said that "a sound came from heaven like the rush of a mighty wind." The house was filled with the noise. Such was the power of the experience that it seemed tongues of flame settled over the disciples' heads. In

this moment, they received the gift of the Holy Spirit—God with them in a fresh, wonderful way.

Fire is a good symbol for what God does through his Holy Spirit. Fire burns away impurities. It inspires us with awe. It gives power. It causes us to be warm.

The flame symbolizing the Holy Spirit has seven tongues. Each tongue stands for a gift of the Holy Spirit. Some detective work is needed to see how this came about. The writer of Revelation 4:5 pictures seven torches burning before the throne of God. He identifies them with seven spirits of God. This is probably the basis for the number seven. Paul writes about the gifts of the Spirit in I Corinthians 12, although the gifts number more than seven. The church apparently associated the seven torches with the flaming tongues of the Pentecost story (Acts 2), moving on to remember the gifts of the Spirit that Paul talked about. What are the gifts of the Spirit symbolized by the seven tongues? Traditionally, two lists have been used to name these gifts. One list is found in Isaiah 11: wisdom, understanding, counsel, might, knowledge, and the fear of the Lord. To make seven gifts, godliness is sometimes added after the fear of the Lord. The other list is from Revelation 5:12. The writer says that the Lamb of God is worthy to receive certain things. They are power, riches, wisdom, strength, honor, glory, and blessing.

Hand of God

THE OLDEST KNOWN SYMBOL FOR God is a hand.

The Old Testament writers recorded their belief that God was the Creator of the world. But they knew God had not just started the world and then left it to run down like a clock. He was the Creator who was everywhere present in his creation, guiding, helping, sustaining his people. When the Old Testament writers wanted to put the feeling of God's closeness and power into language, they used the picture word, hand. This seemed a good way to express the truth of God's action.

When the writer of Deuteronomy wanted to tell how God had rescued the Hebrews from bondage in Egypt, he wrote, "You shall remember that you were a servant in the land of Egypt, and the Lord your God brought you out thence with a mighty hand and an outstretched arm" (Deuteronomy 5:15a). By using the same word picture the prophet Isaiah told people that God could help them, that he heard their prayers:

> Behold, the Lord's hand is
>   not shortened, that it cannot save,
> or his ear dull, that it cannot hear.   (Isaiah 59:1.)

74

But why was the word hand used to express God's closeness and power? Why not foot, or head, or mouth? Because one of the main ways people let each other know they care is with hands. The hands of a mother soothe the baby. An outstretched hand to a stranger means friendship. A hand around a shoulder stands for comradeship or love. Human hands also possess power. Hands make tools, plant crops, and guide boats. A surgeon uses his hands to operate and to help people who are sick.

In Christian art, the hand of God is pictured in three different positions. Each one symbolizes a different truth about God.

In the most familiar picture, a hand extends downward from a cloud. Behind the hand is a circle, which stands for divinity. When we look at this form of the hand, we think of God's creative power which surrounds the universe, and which called it into being. If we wanted to match a text from the Bible with this picture, the beginning verses of Genesis would be good: "In the beginning God created the heavens and the earth. The earth was without form and void, and darkness was upon the face of the deep; and the Spirit of God was moving over the face of the waters."

In another picture the hand is again extended downward, holding five people. This is based on a passage from the Book of Wisdom (a book written by the Hebrews but not included in our Old Testament) which reads: "The souls of the righteous are in the hand of God." God cares and loves each person he has created. We never fall out of his hand. Jesus had the same idea when he said, "Are not five sparrows sold for two pennies? And not one of them is forgotten before God. Why, even the hairs of your head are all numbered. Fear not; you are of more value than many sparrows." (Luke 12:6-7.)

Finally, the hand of God is pictured upright, with the fingers crossed in benediction. When the early Christians saw this symbol, they were reminded of their Master, because the fingers were held in a way that represented an abbreviated spelling of the name "Jesus Christ" in the Greek language.

All-Seeing Eye

ONE OF THE SYMBOLS OF GOD IS AN eye placed in a triangle. It is called the All-Seeing Eye.

The symbol has been in the church since the sixteenth century. Churches in Great Britain put the symbol on the wall directly behind the pulpit. It served to remind the congregation that God comes to us through the preached Word. It also symbolized the Presence of God in worship.

Some people do not like this symbol. They are afraid that the All-Seeing Eye may give us a wrong idea of God. When the symbol was first used, people were taught that God was searching out their sins and would punish them for each and every sin. God does not like for us to sin because it hurts us. He wants us to love and serve him. But he is not a cruel God who delights in finding out our sins and punishing us for them.

When we learn to see God as the loving Father of Jesus Christ, the All-Seeing Eye becomes a symbol of comfort, not fear. God sees when we are in trouble and acts to help us. God sees when we fail and encourages us. God sees when we sin and forgives us when we ask him.

Jesus told about a God who was interested in each person. We need not be anxious, because God loves and cares for us.

The All-Seeing Eye ought to recall these words of Jesus from the sixth chapter of Matthew:

Therefore I tell you, do not be anxious about your life, what you shall eat or what you shall drink, nor about . . . what you shall put on. Is not life more than food, and the body more than clothing? Look at the birds of the air; they neither sow nor reap nor gather into barns, and yet your heavenly Father feeds them. Are you not of more value than they? And which of you by being anxious can add one cubit to his span of life? And why are you anxious about clothing? Consider the lilies of the field, how they grow; they neither toil nor spin; yet I tell you, even Solomon in all his glory was not arrayed like one of these. But if God so clothes the grass of the field which today is alive and tomorrow is thrown into the oven, will he not much more clothe you, O men of little faith? Therefore do not be anxious.

Symbols of the Trinity

CHRISTIANS THINK OF GOD IN three ways. We have know him as the Creator, who made and sustains the world. We have also seen that he has come to us in Jesus Christ, to save us from our sins. Finally, we feel that God is present with us now, giving us strength to be his disciples. This threefold experience of God is often called the Trinity. We believe that God has made himself known in these three ways: Father, Son, and Holy Spirit. We do not worship three gods, but One God who has a threefold nature.

There are many symbols of the Trinity. Perhaps the best known is the triangle. A triangle is a figure constructed of three equal sides. This represents that Father, Son, and Holy Spirit are three equal parts of God's nature. One is no more important than the other.

Sometimes the triangle has the word *Sanctus* on each of the three sides. The word *Sanctus* is a Latin word meaning "holy." When this symbol is used, we think of the holiness, purity, and majesty of each expression of God.

Circles are also used for the Trinity. Three circles overlapping stand for Father, Son, and Holy Spirit. A circle has no beginning and no end. When used alone, it is a symbol for the eternity of God.

A Trefoil is often seen in churches. It is almost the same symbol as the three overlapping circles. The only difference is that the overlapping lines are left out.

Another symbol for the Trinity is called a Triquetra. This is made by placing arcs of a circle together in a design. The center of the Triquetra forms a triangle, which we have seen is another Trinity symbol. The arcs are of equal size, symbolizing the equality of each expression of God's nature. This is a beautiful design.

A green plant is a favorite symbol of the Trinity. The plant is called the Irish shamrock because it grows in Ireland. About four hundred years after Jesus lived on the earth, one of his missionaries named Patrick appeared before the pagan king Ardri. Patrick told the king about the Christian belief in the Trinity. The king was confused and angry.

"What you say is unbelievable!" he said. "How could three Persons be One?"

Patrick stooped and picked a shamrock from the ground. Showing the little plant to the king, he asked, "Is there one leaf or three?"

"I cannot say," the king said.

"Then, if you cannot understand the mystery of the tiny shamrock, you cannot expect to understand the mystery of the Trinity," Patrick replied.

The fleur-de-lis, or iris, can also represent the Trinity. For many years this flower design was the symbol of the royal household of France. The flour-de-lis is a common design on dresses and jewelry. Its many combinations of three make the iris a fine Trinity symbol.

Stars

FROM THE BEGINNING OF TIME, MAN has been fascinated with stars. Some people believe stars influence the future. In some countries when a baby was born it was the custom to call for an astrologer. The astrologer would read the stars and tell the future of the baby—whether he would be rich or poor, coward or hero.

In Christian art, stars are used to refer to the promised coming of Christ, as well as to symbolize God, the Holy Spirit, and the disciples.

After Jesus was born in Jerusalem, wise men from the east followed a star to where he lay. This star, represented as five-pointed, is called the Star of Bethlehem, the Star of Jacob, or the Star of Epiphany. The word "Epiphany" means "showing forth." Some churches observe the season of Epiphany twelve days after Christmas. Early in the church's life, the visit of the wise men symbolized God's showing himself to all the world in the Christ Child. During Epiphany season, these churches remember the visit of the wise men and dedicate themselves anew to telling the good news throughout the world. Epiphany is a great missionary season. The star is actually a symbol of Epiphany, and not Christmas.

A star which stands for God the Father has six points. Often, this star is found in Jewish temples. When used in Jewish temples, it is known as the "Star of David." Many people believe that David's shield was shaped like this star. Christians believe that the six-pointed star is a good symbol for God because each point may be used to remind us of something of his nature: power, wisdom, majesty, love, mercy, and justice.

The Holy Spirit is represented by a seven-pointed star. The Holy Spirit brings good gifts to us. Seven of these gifts are mentioned in the New Testament book of Revelation. Each point of this star stands for the gifts: power, riches, wisdom, strength, honor, glory, and blessing.

There is also a twelve-pointed star. This star stands for the twelve tribes of Israel, or the twelve apostles. For a long time, the number twelve has stood for the closeness of God with man.

Boat

BOATS ARE MENTIONED AGAIN AND again in the New Testament. Jesus called several of his disciples from their fishing boats. Once Jesus got into a boat to preach to the people on shore. At another time, he and the disciples were in a boat when an angry storm caused the waters to toss the ship. Jesus was asleep. The disciples were afraid that the boat would turn over and they would all drown. Awaking Jesus, they said, "Teacher, don't you care that we perish?" With perfect calm, Jesus said, "Peace! Be still!" And the storm ceased. The disciples learned from Jesus that faith overcomes fear. They were safe when they were with Jesus.

The disciples remembered vividly the times Jesus spent in a boat. They recalled also a famous boat in the Old Testament story—the Ark which saved Noah from the Flood. It was not long until the boat symbolized the church. In church the followers of Jesus found that he still spoke, "Peace! Be still!" The church was the ship in which Christians sailed the rough seas of life.

An early document telling how to build churches gave the order that the building should be oblong, toward the east, like a ship. The inside of Gothic churches looks like a ship turned upside down. The word "nave," which is the name given to the main part of the building where the congregation sits, comes from the Latin word *navis* meaning ship. Whenever we see a boat, we are reminded how much we need the church as we try to live as Christians.

Symbols of Baptism

BAPTISM IS THE WAY PEOPLE ARE marked as followers of Christ. There are different beliefs about baptism. Some churches baptize infants because they believe they have a place in the church along with their parents. Other churches believe that baptism should be given only after a person is old enough to understand its meaning. There are two main ways that people are baptized—by sprinkling or immersion. When a person is sprinkled, water is poured on his head by the minister. Baptism by immersion means that the minister immerses the person's whole body in a place filled with water. This place is called a "baptistry." Whatever the method, the minister says, "I baptize you in the name of the Father, Son, and Holy Spirit."

Water itself is a symbol for baptism. There are several good reasons for this. For one thing, we could not have life without water. Water is as necessary to life as the oxygen we breathe. So, baptism marks the new life we have in Jesus Christ. Water is also associated with purifying or cleansing. We wash our hands with water. We bathe with water. Dirty clothes are washed with water. God wants us to be wholly clean—not only our bodies, but also our spirits, minds, and emotions. The waters of baptism stand for God's washing away our impurities and making us clean.

Another symbol for baptism is a dove descending over a bowl of water. The Gospel writers tell us when Jesus was baptized, the Holy Spirit came to him like a dove. When we are baptized, we believe that God's mercy to all men is shown. The dove, which goes quickly from place to place, is a fitting symbol of the Holy Spirit's presence in baptism.

Symbols of
Holy Communion

JESUS AND HIS DISCIPLES HAD gathered for the Passover meal in an upper room somewhere in Jerusalem. It was a few hours before the soldiers would arrest him in the Garden of Gethsemane. During the meal, Jesus took a loaf of bread, broke it, and gave the pieces to his disciples. "This bread stands for my body which will be broken for you," he said. Then he took a cup filled with wine. Passing it around the table, he said, "This wine stands for my blood which will be shed for you."

From that time until now, Christians have observed a meal in remembrance of Jesus' life, death, and resurrection. The meal is known by different names. Sometimes it is called simply "The Lord's Supper." It is known also as the Holy Communion. This meal is a time when Christians come together and feel close to one another because of their faith in Christ. Another name is Eucharist, a Greek word which means thanksgiving. Christians are thankful for what God did for them in Jesus Christ.

The bread and wine symbolize Christ's body and blood. They are visible ways through which Christ comes to us in our worship. Christian art has several symbols of Holy Communion.

Often, they are carved on the communion table or altar, where the bread and wine is placed. Symbols of Holy Communion are based on the stories of the last supper in the first three Gospels.

The cup reminds Christians of the wine Jesus drank. Some churches use a single cup in the service of Holy Communion. The minister gives each person a sip from the cup. Other churches use small individual glasses. Regardless of practice, all churches recognize the cup as a symbol for Holy Communion. The cup is often known as the chalice.

Clusters of grapes stand for the Holy Communion because the wine, or grape juice, used in the service is made from grapes. Twelve bunches of grapes symbolize the apostles.

An ancient chalice, discovered in 1910, is engraved with twelve grape vines along with several grape clusters. The chalice was probably hidden sometime during the Roman persecution of the Christians. This chalice is known as "The Great Chalice of Antioch."

Bread is another symbol of the

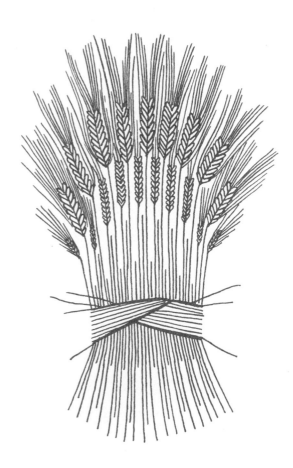

Lord's Supper. Jesus broke bread, and gave it to his disciples. Bread stands for his body. Most churches use very small pieces of bread in the service of Communion. However, a single loaf of bread is used in many churches. The minister tears pieces from the loaf when he serves the people. The single loaf stands for the oneness we have in Christ. As Paul said, "Because there is one bread, we who are many are one body, for we all partake of the one bread." (I Corinthians 10:17.)

Since bread is made from wheat, a sheaf of wheat also symbolizes the Lord's Supper. Wheat, too, stands for Christ's body. Both bread and wheat make us think of Jesus' words, "I am the bread of life; he who comes to me shall not hunger, and he who believes in me shall never thirst" (John 6:35). This means that our relationship with Christ is deeply satisfying.

Symbols
of the Bible

THE BIBLE IS THE MOST IMPORTANT library of books in the world for Christians. In the Bible, we discover God's plan for us. We see how God dealt with the Israelites in mercy and love. We read of the heroes of our faith — David, Amos, Isaiah, Paul, and a host of others. Through the Bible, we learn about God's love shown in Jesus Christ.

There are two symbols of the Bible: an open book and a lamp.

An open book symbolizes that God wants us to read his Word and guides us in understanding what it says to us. The Bible should be opened, and not closed. We should be studying it carefully to find out what God is like and what he wants us to be. The open book also says that the Bible can be read by millions of people over the world. The Bible has been translated in more than a thousand tongues.

A lamp also represents the Bible. A lamp helps us to see when it is dark. A lamp is a sign for study and learning. Christians believe that they learn about God when they study the Bible. It sheds light on our lives. The lamp which is used as a symbol for the Bible is the oldest kind of lamp we know of. The lamp also refers to a quotation from Psalms 119:105:

Thy word is a lamp to my feet
and a light to my path.

Gospel Writers

CARVED IN STONE JUST OVER THE entrance to one of the most beautiful churches in the Southwestern United States—First Presbyterian Church in Wichita Falls, Texas—are a winged man, a winged lion, a winged ox, and an eagle.

These are the symbols for the Gospel writers. Placing them over the church door serves to show the church's debt to these books of the Bible. Without the Gospels, we would not have the story of Jesus. We would not know his teachings. We would not know how he healed and helped people. Christians are thankful for the Gospel writers, the tellers of the good news.

The origin of these symbols is very old. They are based on a verse from the book of Revelation. The writer was describing a vision he had of heaven. He saw a throne. Among those around the throne were "four living creatures, full of eyes in front and behind: the first living creature like a lion, the second living creature like an ox, the third living creature with the face of a man, and the fourth living creature like a flying eagle." (Revelation 4:6-7.) The writer of Revelation was not thinking of the Gospel writers. He was poetically describing the glory of heaven. But the early Christians, on reading this verse, thought back to the Gospel writers. The message of each Gospel seemed to be related to each of the "living creatures."

The symbol for Matthew is a winged man. His Gospel begins with the family history of Jesus, tracing it through the Bible. Matthew dwells more on the humanity of Jesus than any of the other Gospels.

Mark is represented by a winged lion. The lion refers to the opening verses of the Gospel which tell about "the voice of one crying in the wilderness." The lion and the wilderness go together. The lion also symbolizes royalty, and stands for the Kingship of Christ.

A winged ox stands for Luke. The Jews sacrificed an ox in their worship. The Gospel of Luke treats very fully the sacrifice of Jesus Christ on the cross.

98

The Gospel of John is symbolized by an eagle. The eagle is believed to soar higher than any other bird. John writes about Jesus in such a way as to emphasize his closeness with God, the Father. John's book soars like an eagle in describing the Kingship of Jesus. Listen to the way he begins: "In the beginning was the Word, and the Word was with God, and the Word was God. . . . And the Word became flesh and dwelt among us, full of grace and truth; we have beheld his glory, glory as of the only Son from the Father. (John 1:1, 14.)

A leaf having four foils—known as a quatrefoil—also stands for the Gospel writers. Sometimes four quatrefoils make up a larger design, and a winged creature is placed in each leaf.

Shields of the Apostles

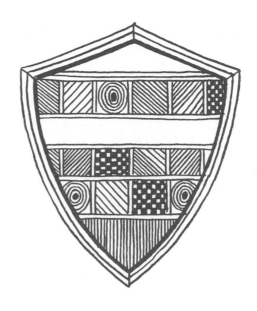

THE FIRST TWELVE FOLLOWERS OF Jesus are known as apostles. This word, apostle, comes from a Greek word which means sent. Every Christian is an apostle because he is sent by his Lord to tell the good news of God's love for the world. However, the first apostles hold a special place in the church. Twentieth-century apostles remember the first-century apostles with thanksgiving for their faith and courage.

Long ago, symbols were developed for each of the twelve original followers of Jesus. Usually, an apostle's symbol appears on a shield. The shield was part of the equipment a soldier in the ancient world carried. It was a large piece of metal which protected him from the arrows and swords of the enemy. Perhaps placing the apostles' symbols on shields serves to remind us that they were soldiers of Christ, who were fighting against evil and injustice. The shield also stresses their soldier-like bravery in spreading the Gospel.

In this chapter, we will learn about these shields. We will recount what the New Testament says about the apostles. We will also read some of the stories that were told about the apostles after Jesus' resurrection. Unlike the biblical accounts of their lives, these stories are products of imaginative minds and have little basis in actual fact. In telling these legends, early Christians sought to honor the apostles and to show the strength of their character. A scholar named William Barclay collected the more familiar stories in a book titled *The Master's Men*. The legends in this chapter, although in briefer form, are based on the Barclay collection.

On the shield of Peter are two crossed keys and a Latin cross turned upside down. Both of these symbols come from events in his life. One event is found in the sixteenth chapter of Matthew. Jesus asked his followers who people said he was. They told Jesus what they had heard: "Some say John the Baptist, others say Elijah, and others Jeremiah or one of the prophets." Jesus asked them, "Who do you say that I am?" Peter said, "You are the Christ, the Son of the living God." Peter believed that Jesus was more than another prophet. Jesus was the One chosen by God to save Israel—he was the Christ. Jesus was glad that Peter had faith in him as the Christ.

He said, "You are Peter, and on this rock, I will build my church." We believe that this means on the rock of Peter's confession of faith, and not on Peter himself. Then, Jesus went on to say, "I will give you the keys of the kingdom of heaven." It is difficult to understand what this means. Perhaps Jesus is saying that he delivers to his apostles the truth about life, the keys to life. Since this word was addressed to Peter, the keys appear on his shield.

The Latin cross turned upside down is based on the writings of Eusebius, an early church historian. Eusebius tells us that Peter went to Rome in 61 A.D. His preaching angered powerful Roman officials, and he was condemned to death. His friends warned him to run for his life. But as Peter was leaving the city, he saw the Lord entering Rome. "Lord," Peter said, "whither goest thou?" The Lord answered, "I am going to Rome to be crucified." Peter understood that Jesus was going to Rome to bear the cross from which he was running away. And so he returned to die. Eusebius says that Peter's wife was crucified before his eyes. He faced the death of his wife and his own death with such courage that the Roman jailer accepted the Christian faith. When the soldiers came to lead him to death, Peter said, "I want to be crucified head downward. I am not worthy to die in the same way as my Lord." His wish was granted.

James, often called James the Greater, was the son of Zebedee and brother of John. James is represented by three scallop shells. The shells stand for his missionary journeys. Sometimes a sword is pictured with a single scallop shell because James was beheaded by the command of Herod. The Gospel records show that along with his brother John, and Peter, he was closer to Jesus than the other apostles. He and his brother John were nicknamed "sons of thunder" because of their quick temper. Both were fishermen.

James and John most often are

mentioned together. James is mentioned by himself only once in the New Testament. A brief sentence in Acts tells of James's death (Acts 12: 1-2). James was the first of the original apostles to become a martyr—to suffer death because of his beliefs.

There exists a legend that James preached in Spain before he was killed and that his body was returned to Spain after his death. Many people believe that he is buried under the cathedral of Santiago de Compostela, a city in the northwestern part of Spain. Spaniards regard James as their patron saint.

107

The shield of John, the brother of James, pictures a chalice and a serpent. This symbol is based on a legend in which a pagan priest gave John poisoned wine to drink. John made the sign of the cross over the chalice. The poison became a serpent and crawled out of the chalice. This story, although not true, does serve to remind us that John escaped a martyr's death. Other than Thaddeus, he is the only one of the apostles who did not die violently.

John was a brave leader in the early church. In his younger days, he traveled with Peter. He was exiled to an island, Patmos, off the coast of Greece. Most of his later years were spent in Ephesus. Clement of Alexandria tells a story about John which demonstrates his courage. Once John rode into a camp of dangerous robbers to find a young Christian whom he had known. The young Christian had left the church to become the

leader of the band of robbers. The robbers surrounded John, but without fear he asked to be taken to their chief. When the young man saw John, he was ashamed and ran. But John chased him and asked him to change his life. Repentant, the young man knelt before John. John said, "The Lord forgives you and wants you back in the church." The young man came back to the church and became a leader in the local congregation.

The shield of Andrew, Peter's brother, carries an X-shaped cross. It is said that Andrew died in the town of Patras in Greece. To make him suffer longer, his enemies bound him to the cross. He lived for several days, dying at last of thirst and exposure. Like his brother Peter, Andrew felt unworthy to be crucified in the same way as Jesus. He asked to be crucified on an X-shaped cross. This type of cross is called a Saint Andrew's cross in honor of the courageous apostle. Because he was martyred in Greece, Andrew is the patron saint of that country.

Andrew is also the patron saint of Russia. It is thought that he preached in an area which is now part of Russia.

In addition to Greece and Russia, Andrew is the patron saint of Scotland. The Scots' flag has a white Saint Andrew's cross on a blue background representing the sky. The story behind this standard dates back eight hundred years after Jesus' birth. There is a legend that a monk named Regulus took some of Andrew's bones with him on a missionary journey to Scotland. He settled on the east coast of Scotland where the town of Saint Andrews now stands. The ruins of Regulus' Church still stand there. The king of the Picts, Hungus, was doing battle with the English. The legend has it that Andrew appeared to Hungus in a dream and assured him of victory. The next day, a shining X-shaped cross appeared in the sky above the army of the Picts. The English were frightened by the shining cross. The Picts cried out as they went into battle, "Saint Andrew, our patron, be our guide!"

Two loaves of bread and a cross is the most familiar symbol for Philip. One day, five thousand people gathered to hear Jesus preach. Seeing the great crowd, Jesus turned to Philip and asked, "How are we to buy bread, and see that these people may eat?" Philip said, "Two hundred denarii would not buy enough bread for each of them to get a little." A denarius—about twenty cents in our money—was a working man's pay for a day. Two hundred denarii was a lot of money, almost a year's wages. Andrew told Jesus that a boy had five barley loaves and two fish, but Andrew didn't see that such a small amount would help much. Jesus asked for everyone to sit down. Then he distributed the loaves and the

fishes. The multitude was fed. The loaves of bread on Philip's shield recall Philip's presence at the feeding of the five thousand. Philip, like Jesus, was interested in feeding the hungry crowd. The cross on the shield does not stand for the way Philip died. It signifies that he followed the way of the cross.

Philip was a missionary at heart. After he was called by Jesus, Philip went to tell his friend Nathanael that he had found the Christ, Jesus of Nazareth. Nathanael didn't believe him. Nazareth was such a small, dirty town. "Can anything good come out of Nazareth?" Nathanael laughed.

Philip did not waver. He invited his friend, "Come and see."

James, the son of Alpheus, often is represented by a saw. According to tradition, when he was ninety-six years old, enemies of the church threw him from the top of the temple. Not satisfied with his death, they showed their hatred by sawing his body apart. Very little else is known of this James. He is often called James the Less, while the other apostle James, the brother of John, is called James the Greater. Since he was the son of Alpheus, James the Less was probably Matthew's brother.

The shield of Thomas contains a vertical spear and a carpenter's square. Many believe that Thomas went to India and built a church with his own hands. The carpenter's square stands for this work. No one knows whether Thomas actually preached in India. However, in South India there is a church which is named "The Christians of St. Thomas." The people believe that their church was started by Thomas.

The vertical spear recalls the way Thomas was supposed to have died. After he had preached and organized churches in India, he went on to China where he was very successful in his work. Then, he returned to India, to a town called Mailapore. The pagan religious leaders grew jealous of his success. They persuaded the people to stone him. He was finally killed by a spear.

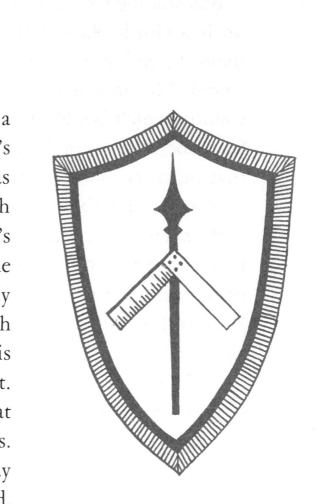

Bartholomew's shield has pictured on it a single flaying knife. Some-times, three knives are shown on the shield. He preached in Armenia, a country which bordered on the Black Sea. The Armenian Church believes that he is its founder. He was killed at Albana. Bartholomew preached with such power that the people turned from their pagan gods and began to follow Jesus Christ. The king and others were baptized. The pagan priests planned Bartholomew's death. The priests plotted with the king's brother Astyages. He had Bartholomew arrested and flayed with knives.

Three purses symbolize Matthew, reminding us of his one-time occupation as a tax collector. In the days of Jesus, tax collectors were among the most hated men in society. The taxes went to support the Romans who had taken over the land of Israel. Some Jews, trying to make the best of things, joined with the Romans. They got some of the tax money as their salary. But they were hated by their fellow Jews, and were not even allowed to attend worship.

Such an outcast was Matthew. One day, he was surprised to hear a voice speaking his name. He looked up and recognized the teacher Jesus of Nazareth. "Follow me," Jesus said. Matthew sat, startled. Jesus wanted him, a tax collector? He could hardly believe his ears. Again, Jesus said, "Follow me." Matthew's heart beat faster. Jesus was inviting him to a new life. Matthew left the tax table and followed Jesus.

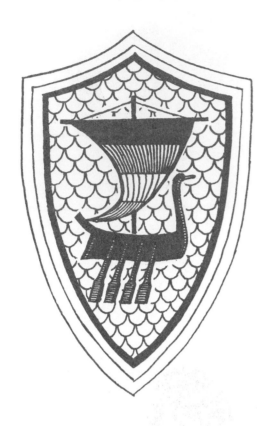

A sailing ship is on the shield of Thaddeus. The ship stands for his missionary journeys. The Armenian church believes that he, along with Bartholomew, brought Christianity to that country. He is also said to have preached in Syria, Arabia, and Mesopotamia. We know little about Thaddeus' life. The Gospels speak of him by three different names. Mark calls him Thaddeus. Matthew calls him Lebbeus, whose last name was Thaddeus. Luke names him Judas, the brother of James.

Simon the Zealot has a fish lying on a book for his symbol. When Jesus called the disciples, he often said, "Come, and I will make you fishers of men." Their job was to help people by bringing them into fellowship with Christ. The fish stands for Simon as a "fisher of men." The book symbolizes the Gospel—the good news about Jesus—which the early Christians wrote down on papyrus scrolls.

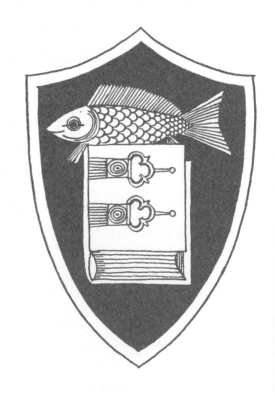

Calling Simon a Zealot meant that he was a member of a group of Israelites who wanted to drive the Roman conquerors out of the country by force. The Zealots were a band of fierce fighters. Jesus did not believe in hurting other people, even in self-defense. Perhaps he chose Simon as a member of the twelve to teach him that the way of peace was better than the way of war.

There was one other original apostle. His name was Judas Iscariot. Judas was also a Zealot. He believed Jesus was going to conquer Rome and set up an earthly kingdom. He did not understand Jesus' way of peace. Many believe that when Judas betrayed Jesus to the Romans, he did so with the thought that he would force Jesus to use his great powers against Rome. When Jesus allowed himself to be crucified instead, Judas realized his terrible mistake. Remorseful, he hanged himself (Matthew 27: 5). A different account of Judas' death is given in Acts 1:18-19. His story is one of the most tragic in all of history. His name has become a symbol of betrayal and deceit. Because he betrayed Jesus, the church gave him no symbol. Sometimes a blank shield representing Judas is shown along with the other apostles.

After the death and resurrection of Jesus, the apostles chose Matthias to succeed Judas. On his shield are an ax and a Bible. Tradition says that he was beheaded for preaching the Gospel. Not much is known about his missionary activity, but it is believed that he wrote a book titled *The Traditions of Matthias.*

When the shields of the apostles are displayed the shield of Paul is usually added. Although not one of the original twelve, Paul was the most famous of the early missionaries.

Paul, a Jew, was at first a persecutor of Christians. He was present when Stephen, the first Christian martyr, was stoned to death. He went from town to town in an effort to find Christians and get them to change their faith. As he was going to Damascus one day, he saw a vision of Jesus. Paul realized that he had been mistaken to persecute the Christians. He asked for forgiveness and joined the church.

121

Paul traveled and organized churches in such towns as Corinth, Philippi, Thessalonica, and Ephesus. The New Testament contains some of his letters to these churches. He is called the apostle to the Gentiles because he believed that Jesus Christ should be preached to everyone, not only the Jews. Paul underwent suffering and danger as a missionary. He was a prisoner in Rome, and finally, the Roman emperor Nero ordered him to be beheaded.

The shield of Paul contains an open Bible and sword. The sword stands for the Word of God as the "Sword of the Spirit." The Latin words on the Bible, *Spiritus Gladius,* mean "Sword of the Spirit."

The World
Is Full of Signs

SOME OF THE MAJOR CHRISTIAN
symbols have been examined in this
book. There are many more. Symbols
have helped Christians of every age
to live their faith with courage.
When we enter a church building,
we must be aware of these signs. It is
helpful to be still and think about what they mean.

The world is full of symbols and signs. God planned so that
no matter where we are we may be reminded of his love and
care. God's greatness is seen in the mountains stretching to the
skies, in heavens filled with stars, in the oceans rolling out of
sight over the horizon. God's care for detail is shown in flowers,
in blades of grass, and in the complexity of the human body.
A hymn by Maltbie D. Babcock expresses this truth:

> This is my Father's world.
> The birds their carols raise,
> The morning light, the lily white,
> Declare their maker's praise.
> This is my Father's world:
> He shines in all that's fair;
> In the rustling grass, I hear him pass,
> He speaks to me everywhere.

There are signs in the city also. The city's skyscrapers, bridges, freeways, libraries, hospitals, parks, homes, and schools, symbolize man cooperating with God to create. God is found in nature, untouched by our human hands, but he is found also in the hustle of the city streets where men go about their work.

We have seen that Christianity's symbols grew out of the Bible's word pictures. Christian symbols form only a small part of the wonderful world of signs which God has given us. Everything in the world points to God as Creator and Sustainer. We rejoice in the magnificent signs of the world.

Index
to Symbols